zendoodle colorscapes

Love Thy Neighbor

A Coloring Book
of Faith and Grace

CASTLE POINT BOOKS
NEW YORK

You are the light
of the world.

Matthew 5:14

Beloved, let us love
one another,
for love is from God;
and everyone who
loves is born of God
and knows God.

1 John 4:7

COME NEAR
TO GOD
AND HE WILL
COME NEAR
TO YOU.

James 4:8

For the Spirit
God gave us
does not make us
timid,
but gives us
power,
love and
self-discipline.
2 Timothy 1:7

LOVE

Love is patient,
love is kind.
It does not envy, it does not boast, it is not proud.
It is not rude, it is not self-seeking,
it is not easily angered,
it keeps no record of wrongs.
Love does not delight in evil
but rejoices with the truth.
It always protects,
always trusts,
always hopes,
always perseveres.

LOVE never fails.

I Corinthians 13:4-8

Let love be without dissimulation. Abhor that which is evil; cleave to that which is good

Romans 12:9

Let brotherly love continue

Hebrews 13:1

Because thy loving kindness is better than life

Psalm 63:3

Be Wise
and guide thine heart
in the way
Proverbs 23:19

DO
JUSTICE
LOVE KINDNESS
WALK
HUMBLY

Micah 6:8

A merry heart maketh a cheerful countenance

Proverbs 15:13

AS THE FATHER HATH LOVED ME,
SO HAVE I LOVED YOU:

Continue ye in my Love

John 15:9

If you love me, keep my commandments. John 14:15

His Beloved

PSALM 127:2

A friend loveth at all times ♥

Proverbs 17:17

And ye shall seek me, and find me, when ye shall search for me with all your heart.

Jeremiah 29:13

Beloved, let us love one another: for love is of God; and every one that loveth is born of God, and knoweth God.

1 John 4:7

Love beareth all things

1 Corintians 13:7

BE KIND BE PATIENT BE LOVING

Be renewed in the spirit of your mind.
Eph. 4:23

When I love you
I am loving me
because we
are one.

Ephesians 5:28

Act in such a matter that you are living proof of a loving God.

FOR GOD SO LOVED THE WORLD, THAT HE GAVE
HIS ONLY BEGOTTEN SON, THAT WHOSOEVER
BELIEVETH IN HIM SHOULD NOT PERISH, BUT HAVE
EVERLASTING LIFE. JOHN 3:16

For the LORD is good; his mercy is everlasting; and his truth endureth to all generations.

HIS love endures forever

Psalm 100:5

AND ABOVE ALL THESE THINGS PUT ON CHARITY,
WHICH IS THE BOND OF PERFECTNESS. COL. 3:14

Be devoted to one another in love.
Honor one another above yourselves.
Romans 12:10

And we have known and believed the love that God hath to us. God is love; and he that dwelleth in love dwelleth in God, and God in him.

1 John 4:16

Greater love hath no man than this, that a man lay down his life for his friends. John 15:13

For God hath not given us the spirit of fear; but of power, and of love, and of a sound mind.

2 Timothy 1:7

I WiLL rUN the Way oF thy coMMaNdMeNtS, WHeN thoU SHaLt eNLarge My Heart. PSaLM 119:32

Let the peace of God rule in your hearts

Colossians 3:15

He brought me to the banqueting house and His banner over me was LOVE

Song of Solomon 2:4

And to know the love of Christ, which passeth knowledge, that ye might be filled with the fulness of God.

Ephesians 3:19

LOVE HOPETH ALL THINGS

1 Corinthians 13:7

LOVE is KIND

Never fails ♥ Always trusts ♥ Always hopes ♥ It keeps no records of wrongs ♥ It is not self-seeking ♥ It is not proud ♥

1 Corinthians 13:4-13

Love
endureth
all
things

1 Corinthians 13:7

My heart rejoiceth in the Lord

1 Samuel 2:1

Serve one another in love

Galatians 5:13

I have found the one whom my soul loves

Song of Solomon 3:4

If we love one another, God dwelleth in us, and his love is perfected in us. 1 John 4:12